Feb. 22, 2010

CARS

ESCALADE

Michael Bradley

 Marshall Cavendish
Benchmark
New York

Marshall Cavendish Benchmark
99 White Plains Road
Tarrytown, NY 10591
www.marshallcavendish.us

All websites were available and accurate when this book was sent to press.

Library of Congress Cataloging-in-Publication Data

Bradley, Michael, 1962-
  Escalade / by Michael Bradley.
    p. cm. — (Cars)
  Includes index.
  ISBN 978-0-7614-4101-4
  1. Escalade sport utility vehicle—Juvenile literature. I. Title.
  TL230.5.E785 B73 2010
  629.223 22—dc22
  2008031461

Editor: Megan Comerford
Publisher: Michelle Bisson
Art Director: Anahid Hamparian
Series Designer: Daniel Roode

Photo research by Connie Gardner

Cover photo by Ron Kimball/www.kimballstock.com

The photographs in this book are used by permission and through the courtesy of:
Ron Kimball/www.kimballstock.com: 1, 18, back cover; *GM Media Archive:* 10, 11, 16, 19, 28; *Landov:* UPI
Photos/General Motors, 4; *AP Photo:* Paul Saneya, 6; Kiichiro Sato, 7; Damian Dovarganes, 8;
Anja Niedringhaus, 9; Stefano Paltera, 20; Matrial Trezzini, 29; *Alamy:* pbp galleries, 13; Emil Pozarill, 14;
Bill Philpot, 15; evox, 21; *Getty Images:* Arnold Turner, 23; Mark Elias, 26; *Corbis:* Mario Anzunoi, 24;
Car Culture, 25.

Printed in Malaysia
1 3 5 6 4 2

CONTENTS

Singer and actress Jennifer Hudson struts down the runway in front of a 2007 Escalade at the GM TEN event in Los Angeles, California. Celebrities of all types are attracted to the flashy SUV.

CHAPTER ONE

STAR POWER

Even with high gas prices and Americans' efforts to save energy, few people expected to see Cadillac joining the cause. Not with its Escalade, at least. The big **SUV** (sport-utility vehicle) had become a symbol of **status** and **luxury**, just as Cadillacs had always been. But the Escalade was different. Bigger. Sure, General Motors, which owned Cadillac, had talked about an Escalade **hybrid**, but few people believed the **hype.** Could the company that had been identified with size, power, and wealth go green?

You bet. And there it was, right on the red carpet at GM's 2007 Academy Awards pre-party. Jennifer Hudson, who would win an Oscar for *Dreamgirls* later that night, led the way down the red carpet, but all eyes were on what followed. It was an Escalade, the perfect **accessory** for a collection of stars. But this wasn't just any Escalade. Those who paid close attention noticed stickers on the SUV that said "hybrid." GM hadn't been joking a year earlier when it announced the Escalade would be joining the hybrid club with a vehicle that gets eight more miles per gallon than the standard model. And what better way for Cadillac to make news than when surrounded by celebrities?

The Escalade has been red-carpet ready since the beginning. Okay, maybe not the very beginning, because the first few years

Hines Ward, wide receiver for the Pittsburgh Steelers, was awarded a Cadillac after being named MVP of Super Bowl XL in 2006. Of course he went for the Escalade!

Many people, especially celebrities, like to have special rims put on their Escalades. The rim is the inside part of the wheel on which the tire is mounted. Cadillac offers several different rim designs to its Escalade customers.

of the SUV's life were a little rocky. But growing pains are normal for everything. Once GM got it right, the Escalade became a symbol of class and elegance, all wrapped up in a powerful package. The Escalade was a true **phenomenon** that **appealed** to suburban families, as well as celebrities from the worlds of movies, music, and sports.

No one should have been surprised when Cadillac nailed it. The company had been creating cars for America's best and brightest for more than a hundred years. Presidents, movie stars, athletes, singers, and captains of industry had turned to Cadillac to satisfy their automotive needs. They wanted comfort, style, and the kind of **upscale** extras they felt they deserved. When it came time to enter the SUV arena, Cadillac did so perfectly. Not only did the Escalade keep the company's **reputation** for high-end products intact, it also appealed to younger drivers. That was new. Cadillac had traditionally appealed to older, successful people.

But when rap, movie, and sports stars started driving around in their Escalades, the younger generation took notice. If their idols were

The introduction of the Escalade brought a cool factor to Cadillac, whose cars had been historically popular with older generations. Now, young people flock to dealerships to check out the trendy SUV.

General Motors, the company that owns Cadillac, tried to increase sales in Europe by showing off the newest Escalade at the 2006 Geneva International Motor Show in Switzerland.

rocking the 'Slade, then they wanted to, also. Not that the SUV was for everybody. It still carried a pretty hefty price tag. But that didn't stop the kids from dreaming. If they made it big, they would buy a cool ride—an Escalade, of course.

The Escalade's success is impressive for an SUV introduced at the very end of the twentieth century. Cadillac dropped the Escalade on the automotive world in 1999. Within three years, it was a sensation. Whether it was a standard model, which still had enough features to make other SUVs jealous, or a **tricked-out** showpiece, the Escalade was a big deal. Big enough to outshine some of Hollywood's finest stars.

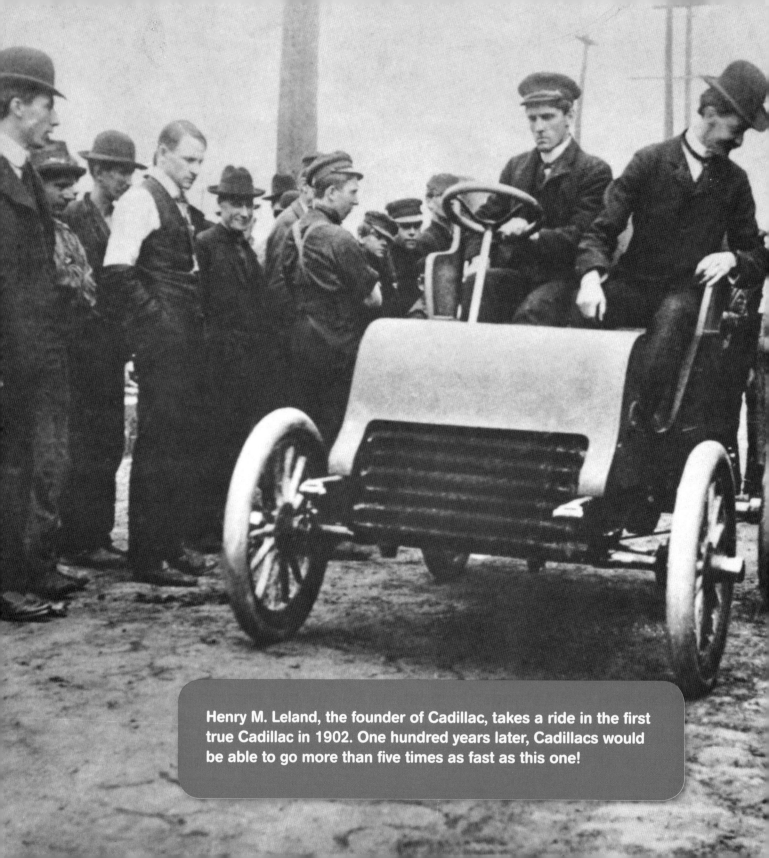

Henry M. Leland, the founder of Cadillac, takes a ride in the first true Cadillac in 1902. One hundred years later, Cadillacs would be able to go more than five times as fast as this one!

From the minute it hit the roads in 1902, the Cadillac was a symbol of top quality and high style. That's how founder Henry Leland wanted it, and it's how things have been ever since.

Leland was born in Vermont in 1843, and as a young man showed an ability to produce quality products and improve on those already in use. During the Civil War, Leland served as a mechanic for the Union Army and developed a reputation for **precise** work. In 1890

Is that really a car?! Cadillac engineers test-drive an engine and car frame in 1915.

he moved to Detroit, Michigan, and started a firm that specialized in making tools and gears for bicycles and, later, steam and combustion engines. His extremely accurate and high-quality products were quite popular.

As the automobile became part of American life, Leland and his company were in high demand. His engines and **transmissions** were found in cars produced throughout Detroit, which was becoming the country's auto capital. Not **content** to only make parts, Leland decided to start his own car company. In 1902, he purchased a building and equipment from Henry Ford's old motor car factory and made his first car. He named it after the founder of Detroit, French explorer and nobleman Antoine de la Mothe Cadillac.

The first Cadillac was introduced on October 17, 1902, and quickly became popular. Leland's attention to detail made the car one of the finest around. And the price tag proved it. By 1904, a Cadillac Model D sold for $2,800 (more than $60,000 today), a large amount of money at the time. But the luxury car market was growing, and people wanted top-shelf vehicles. Leland was happy to provide them. In 1906, Cadillac introduced the Osceola, which had glass windows and curtains in the back window. It sold for $3,000. If you wanted luxury, a Cadillac was the car to get.

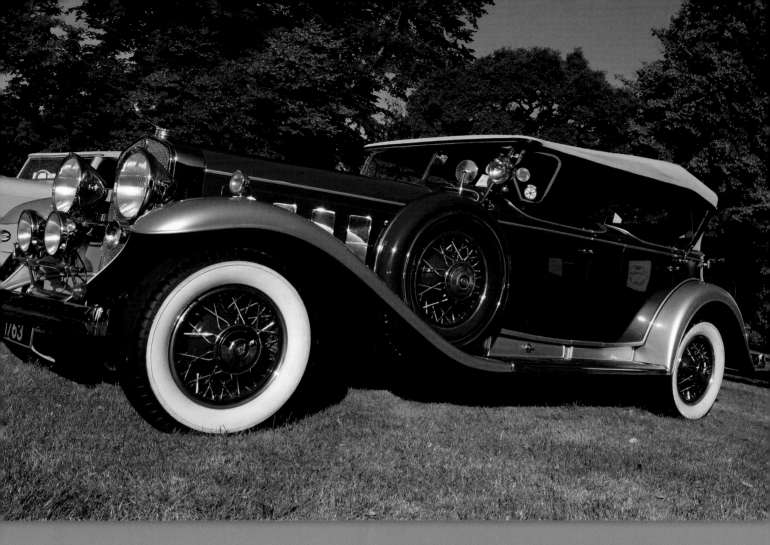

Classic Cadillacs like this 1931 Cadillac 452A are still in high demand. Some are worth more than half a million dollars!

Leland's automobiles were so popular and of such high quality that General Motors wanted to buy the Cadillac company. In 1909, Leland received $500,000 in cash and $5.1 million in GM stock in the largest sale in Detroit Stock Exchange history. The good news was that Leland and his team would continue to run Cadillac, and that meant the cars would continue to be of the highest quality.

Over the next several decades, Cadillac became the "Standard of the World." Its luxury automobiles continued to win praise and loyal customers, all of whom wanted luxury and style. In 1915, Cadillac put V-8 engines in all of its cars, making them the most powerful around. By 1924, Cadillac offered customers five hundred different color combinations, while its competition, such as Lincoln (owned by Ford Motor Company), worked mostly in black. By 1930, the company had

The Cadillac Eldorado, like the 1953 model pictured here, was considered extremely cool and state-of-the-art.

The Cadillac Coup DeVille was a popular car, particularly in the 1950s. Models like this 1959 DeVille have been featured in the movies *Gone in 60 Seconds*, *Kingpin*, and the 2006 Pixar animated film *Cars*.

introduced the V-16 engine, a smooth, quiet power provider. In 1953, the Eldorado **debuted**, giving America more luxury and performance than any other car made in the country.

The **innovations** and excitement continued over the next fifty years. Cadillacs continued to be the standard for luxury in America. The Eldorado and DeVille models were household names and style leaders. When buyers became more interested in smaller cars during the 1970s, Cadillac made the high-end Seville. The CTS and XLR appealed to those who wanted sportier models. And in 1999, in response to Ford Motor Company's popular Lincoln Navigator, Cadillac introduced the Escalade.

The company would never be the same.

The Cadillac Escalade is popular among families because of its roomy interior, but popular among teens and young adults because of its cool look.

CHAPTER THREE

READY FOR THE RED CARPET

By the last years of the twentieth century, the SUV was quickly becoming America's favorite vehicle. Families had room for five—or more—and all their luggage. The trucks rode high and gave drivers a sense of security they didn't have in smaller cars. As the SUV market grew, buyers started calling out for luxury **versions**.

Ford started the luxury SUV movement when it introduced the Lincoln Navigator in 1998. It was more

This 2002 Cadillac Escalade EXT combines the stylish look of the Escalade and the useful flatbed of a pickup truck.

than just a truck; it was style and power blended together, and Americans looking for more than just the basics loved it. Finally, they had an SUV they could bring to the country club.

That didn't sit too well with General Motors, which had worked hard to keep the Cadillac brand at the top of American luxury vehicles. It needed an answer. It needed the Escalade. In 1999, the model debuted, looking more like a pickup truck than a Caddy. But give GM a break. It needed a vehicle to compete with the Navigator, so it created the Escalade quickly. In some ways, it wasn't very different from some of the other SUVs offered by GM. There wasn't any real change in handling, braking, or acceleration. Some criticized its arrival, saying Cadillac had lost its direction.

That was hardly the case. Yes, the Escalade had made a quick run to the **showroom**, but GM's strategy was simple. It would introduce the model in 1999 while working on its next version. That gave drivers a chance to learn about the product while GM perfected it. They didn't even produce a 2001 Escalade. Everything was pointing toward 2002.

This 345-horsepower Vortec 6000 V-8 engine, found in some models of the Escalade, is also used in similar trucks and SUVs, like the Chevy Silverado and the Hummer H2.

And rightly so. When the second generation Escalade hit the market, the critics shut their mouths. This was what everybody had expected from Cadillac. The new Escalade had a V-8 engine that was one of the most powerful in any SUV. And it handled like a sedan instead of a truck. Now everybody could see what engineers at Cadillac could do when they had the time. Not that anybody was surprised. The Cadillac was still the top-of-the-line American car. Now it was also the top luxury truck. It came in two versions, the pickup and the SUV, and both were a step up for Cadillac and the light-truck market.

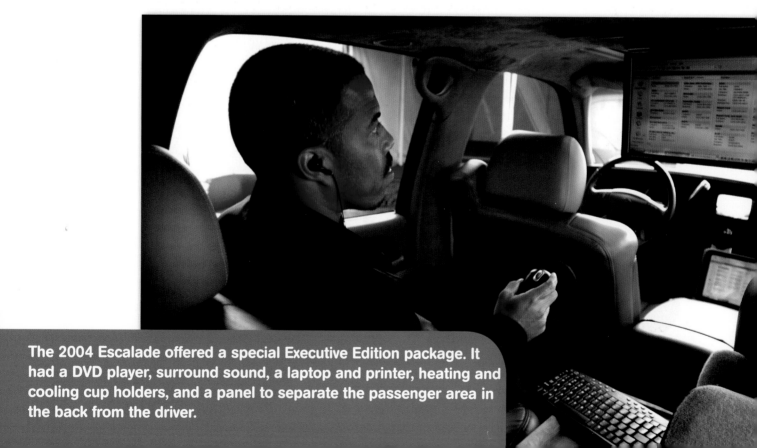

The 2004 Escalade offered a special Executive Edition package. It had a DVD player, surround sound, a laptop and printer, heating and cooling cup holders, and a panel to separate the passenger area in the back from the driver.

New models of the Escalade have a global positioning system (GPS) installed in the dashboard. It is a touch-screen unit with very high resolution. You'll never get lost in your Escalade!

Despite all of its old-style Cadillac **traits**, the 2002 Escalade had another bonus: It was cool. For the first time in its history, Cadillac appealed to a younger market. Sure, kids had always dreamed of some day "making it" and being able to afford a luxury vehicle. But the Escalade sent younger-than-ever drivers to showrooms, with good reason. Not only did the SUV have the ability to perform on the roads, it had a long list of standard features designed to **pamper** the driver. The seats were covered with buttery leather. The wood trim was smooth and shiny. There was hands-free calling and a neighborhood-rattling sound system.

It wasn't perfect yet, but the best was yet to come. As the Escalade continued to grow, it got more and more attention. Pretty soon, it would be more than just a hot new SUV.

It would be a sensation.

CHAPTER FOUR

KING OF BLING

Cadillac **executives** knew they had scored big with the 2002 Escalade. The model was zooming out of showrooms and onto roads. But there was more.

The SUV wasn't just found in mall parking lots and highway lanes. Escalades were in music videos. They were in the driveways of professional athletes' mansions. They were quickly becoming a symbol of wealth and high style throughout America. If you wanted to look cool on the road, you got an Escalade.

For decades, Cadillac had been the car for the mature driver. Before the Escalade, the average Cadillac driver's age was sixty-two. But so many men ages twenty to twenty-nine were buying the Escalade

When Shaquille O'Neal got his 2002 Escalade—dubbed the ShaqMobile—he customized it. It has 20-inch (51-cm) chrome rims, leather seats with the Superman emblem, a couple of subwoofers, and three cameras. Shaq sold it on eBay in 2004.

that the average dropped twelve years. Dealers had to throw teenagers out of their showrooms because the kids would come in after school and spend hours checking out the SUV and dreaming of owning one.

Athletes and rappers did more than dream. They bought. At one point, six players on the NBA's Golden State Warriors owned Escalades. Many of the players took their rides to teammate Chris Mills's **custom** shop to get the full treatment.

The Escalade even rubs shoulders with high fashion. The interior of this Escalade is covered in Louis Vuitton fabric featuring the famous "LV" pattern. It also has a complete entertainment system and glass seats.

Rims. TVs. Video-game systems. The works. By early 2002, at least a dozen rap songs mentioned Escalades. The SUVs were big and comfortable, they rode well, and they looked great with or without customized extras. What started as an effort to compete in the SUV market had become an explosive success for Cadillac.

The fun continued as the decade rolled on, and Cadillac became a pop culture phenomenon, instead of a symbol of status and comfort. In 2005, GM provided a fleet of 130 Escalades for **nominees**, presenters, and other celebrities at the Grammy Awards, which honor

This V-8 hybrid engine is half the system that powers the Escalade Hybrid, released in the summer of 2008. The other half is the electric variable transmission (EVT), which has two electric motors that use energy from the 300-volt battery. This helps wring out a few more miles on each gallon of gas.

General Motors president Troy Clarke unveiled the Escalade Hybrid at the South Florida International Auto Show in 2007. One of the Hybrid's coolest features is an 8-inch (2-cm) touch screen that shows where the power is coming from: the gas engine, the electric motors, or both. Now the Escalade is not only cool, but eco-friendly as well!

the nation's top musical performers. Each Escalade had 20-inch (51-cm) chrome wheels and a fancy steel **grille.** It made sense to let the big names sit in the big ride. In 2004 Cadillac set a record by selling 62,250 Escalades.

More proof of the car's popularity came from a rather unusual statistic. In 2007 the Highway Loss Data Institute reported that more Escalades were stolen from the streets than any other car. No other car's theft rate came close. It wasn't something Cadillac was particularly proud of, but it showed the SUV was in high demand.

Although sales cooled in 2005 and 2006 for all luxury trucks, the Escalade still easily outsold its competitors. But it needed to do more. So, in 2007, Cadillac introduced a bigger, more powerful, smoother Escalade, and it was a beauty. Inside, the comfort and luxury were obvious, even more so than in previous models. If you were looking for the first-place finisher in the SUV category, you went straight to Cadillac, as usual.

But even that wasn't enough. Drivers wanted better gas mileage from their big SUVs, so Cadillac put together the hybrid for 2009. It was just another step from America's high-end leader. For more than one hundred years, Cadillac meant one thing: excellence.

The future appears to be offering more of the same.

Vital Statistics

1999 Escalade

Power: 255 hp
Engine Size: 348 ci/5.7L
Engine Type: Vortec 5700 V-8
Weight: 6,800 lbs (3,084 kg)
Top Speed: 110 mph (177 km/h)
0–60 mph (0–96.5 km/h): 10.5 sec

2009 Escalade Hybrid

SPECIAL FACT:
Gets 21 miles per gallon
(9 km/L) on the highway

Power: 332 hp
Engine Size: 366 ci/6.0L
Battery Power: 300 volts
Engine Type: V-8 LIVC
Weight: 5,708 lbs (2,589 kg)
Top Speed: 106 mph (171 km/h)
0-60 mph (0-96.5 km/h): 8 sec

GLOSSARY

accessory   An object or feature added to increase comfort or beauty.

appeal   To be attractive or interesting to people.

content   Happy and not wanting more.

custom   Something that is made according to a specific order.

debut   The first time something appears in public.

executive   A person in charge of a business.

grille   The front part of a car, usually made of shiny metal, which protects the engine. It is usually designed to make the car look good.

hybrid   A combination of two or more things. A hybrid car runs on a combination of gas and electricity.

hype   Excitement created by lots of advertising.

innovation   A new idea or a new way of doing something.

luxury   Something that provides comfort and pleasure, but is not necessary.

nominee   Something or someone being considered for an award or honor.

pamper   To spoil someone, or treat them with lots of care and attention.

phenomenon   Something that is unusual and extraordinary.

precise   Extremely careful and exact.

reputation   How someone or something is seen by the public.

showroom   The part of an automotive dealership where new cars are displayed for customers to look at them.

status   A high position in society.

SUV   Sport-utility vehicle; a lightweight truck that can tow and carry cargo and also hold up to eight passengers.

trait	A distinct feature.
transmission	the part of an engine that gives power to the wheels, allowing it to change gears, move forward or backward, or go faster.
tricked out	Having lots of extra, often expensive, features.
upscale	Something that is of a high quality and is attractive to wealthy people.
version	One form of a product or idea.

FURTHER INFORMATION

BOOKS

Bonsall, Thomas. *The Cadillac Story: The Postwar Years*. Palo Alto, CA: Stanford General Books, 2003.

Van Bogart, Angelo. *Cadillac: 100 Years of Innovation*. Iola, WI: Krause Publications, 2003.

WEBSITES

www.cadillac.com

www.cadillac.com/EscaladeHybrid

www.edmunds.com/cadillac/escalade/pictures.html

About the Author

MICHAEL BRADLEY is a writer and broadcaster who lives near Philadelphia. He has written for *Sports Illustrated for Kids*, *Hoop*, *Inside Stuff*, and *Slam* magazines and is a regular contributor to Comcast SportsNet in Philadelphia.